Let's Explore Coral Reefs

Michael Patrick O'Neill
Batfish Books

O'Neill, Michael Patrick
Let's Explore Coral Reefs / Michael Patrick O'Neill
ISBN 978-0-9728653-3-3
LCCN 2005901563

Printed in China

Batfish Books
PO Box 32909
Palm Beach Gardens, FL 33420-2909
www.batfishbooks.com
Photographer's Website:
www.mpostock.com

10 9 8 7 6 5 4 3

IF beauty had an address...

Coral Reef; Fiji

It Would be in a Coral Reef,

Where a living rainbow of colorful animals awaits your discovery.

Blue Angelfish

Join me,
Charlie the Crab,
as I explore this
wonderful world in
the clear shallows
of the sea.

Let's go!

Coral Reef; Florida

Cradle of Life

Coral reefs are home to over 4,000 types of fish, 700 species of coral and countless plants and animals.

Found in nearly 100 tropical and sub-tropical countries, coral reefs need clean, clear water to grow.

Cowfish

Clown Triggerfish

HOUSE OF COLOR AND LIGHT

Hawksbill Sea Turtle

GROWING ON ROCK CALLED LIMESTONE, THE CORAL REEF IS A LIVING, UNDERWATER "HOUSE," PAINTED IN A VARIETY OF COLORS.

With time, live plants and animals make this magical house bigger and bigger.

Some coral reefs become so incredibly big that astronauts can see them from space. Imagine!

CoraL ReeF

LiMeSToNe

Coral Reef; Indonesia

Cities in the Sea

The coral, sponges and rock formations attract all sorts of critters.

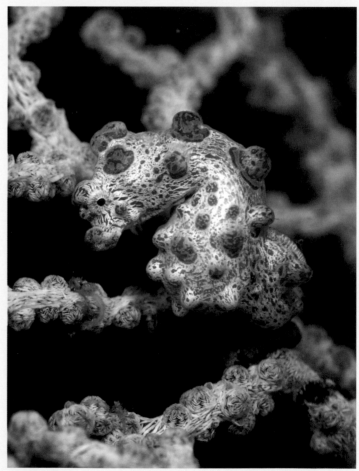

Pygmy Seahorse

Coral reefs are busy underwater communities that never sleep, humming with activity around the clock.

The Day Shift

The majority of animals are active during the day: eating, cleaning, napping and socializing.

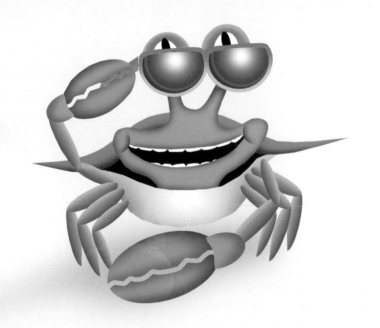

Let's take a look at what some reef animals are up to.

A SCHOOL OF Big-eye Jacks SWirLS iN the SUNSHiNE...

a Queen Angelfish and a French Grunt patrol their neighborhood...

and an ARROW Crab CLeaNS HiS HOMe, an aNeMONe.

The Night Shift

WHEN THE SUN SETS, THE ACTION DOESN'T STOP. WITH MOST FISH ASLEEP, CHARISMATIC CREEPY CRAWLIES ARE ON THE MOVE.

Hidden by darkness, these "night owls" search for food and adventure. Let's meet a few of them.

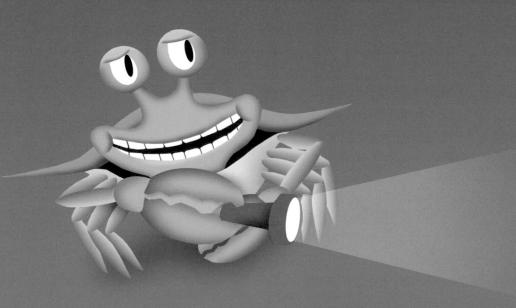

The Star-Eye Hermit Crab explores a sandy patch...

the Octopus peers from his home, an empty bottle...

and a NUDiBRaNCH SeaRCHeS FoR a MaTe at The MidNight HoUR.

THe BOSS

Day or Night, everybody, From cLoWNS to cONCHS to crabS (Like Me!), payS attention to the Tiger SharK, the KiNG OF the coraL reeF.

This is one awesome animal! Nearly 20 ft. long, it has a mouth the size of a big TV, and an appetite to match.

Save Our Seas

Many people depend on coral reefs, and we have to take care of this precious habitat. Otherwise, we'll have a lot of problems down the road.

Besides being a beautiful place to dive and visit, reefs are important to us all.

Let's See Why...

Scuba divers pick up garbage from a coral reef in Florida.

Medicine Maker

Scientists studying coral reefs are making important medical discoveries.

Who would have thought? The cure for some cancers may one day be found inside the seemingly simple sponge.

Several types of sponges can be found on the coral reef.

Food Basket

Fish from coral reefs feed millions of people worldwide. If we take good care of this valuable resource, we will never run out of fish fillets!

In other words, we should never take more than we need.

Blue Marlin

Oriental Sweetlips

A photographer swims with a Goliath Grouper.

Divers' Paradise

Many countries and islands rely on money from tourists, who visit to scuba dive in their clear waters.

Protect the oceans, and they will keep coming! I guarantee it!

Lionfish

Celebrate the Sea

Coral reefs are one of the great wonders of planet Earth. Enjoy and protect them.

Here are four things you can do to help:

1. Get involved in beach clean-ups.

2. Visit your local aquarium and learn about marine animals and ecosystems.

3. Throw all garbage away in the trash – not in the oceans!

4. Don't take live shells or coral from the sea!

Please!

Coral Reef; Fiji

Coral Reef; Fiji